# ANYONE FOR T

*Growing up in Wallington between the Wars*

*by*

**EILEEN WHITEING**

*Design: Shirley Edwards*

London Borough of Sutton Libraries & Arts Services

## AUTHOR'S NOTE

Eventually the desire becomes overwhelming, to set down before it is too late — before the failing memory of old age shrouds for ever — the texture of one's life, even though the writer may not have achieved great fame or fortune. So many autobiographies reflect a very rich or a very poor background, frequently provincial; but mine belongs to the middle-class of the South, for a change, and as I grew up during the legendary Twenties and Thirties I have tried to record an accurate picture of those days, already becoming quite remote. The families of my parents and grandparents spanned nearly a hundred years of continuous residence in Wallington, and it is to their memory that I dedicate my narrative.

*February 1979*

*First published 1979*

© 1979 London Borough of Sutton
Libraries and Arts Services
Central Library, St. Nicholas Way, Sutton, Surrey
Tel: 01-661 5050

ISBN 0 9503224 7 4

*Printed by*
*Dasprint Limited, 159 Brookwood Road, London SW18 5BD*

# TIMES REMEMBERED

*How much of me is still*
*that small shy child*
*who went to school with eager heart*
*too many years ago?*
*Laburnum dripped in gold cascades*
*along the tree-lined paths,*
*and tar was melting on the*
*quiet roads.*
*I learned to read and*
*books became my friends, though*
*music lessons seemed quite hard.*
*I loved my friends and gathered*
*wild flowers in the woods,*
*or fished for crabs in tiny*
*warm sea-pools.*
*Today I write my verse,*
*arrange my flowers, love my friends,*
*and walk beside the summer sea:*
*but life has intervened somehow*
*and blurred the space between,*
*making it not an easy task*
*to find that child again.*

Eileen Whiteing

*The author in her swinging cot, 1912*

*Dr. Cressy, standing (centre) with members of the staff of the old Cottage Hospital, Rochester Road, Carshalton (now Rochester Road Clinic)*

# CHAPTER ONE

## The Early Years

According to my mother, I achieved the distinction of being born at the peak of the week in those days; namely, at the time of mid-day dinner on Sunday, July 7th, 1912. The family doctor was famous locally for his fiery temper and was very displeased at being summoned by the already-resident trained nurse at this particular time on his off-duty Sunday. There was, of course, no question of the mother's being whisked off to a hospital for this event, unless a serious emergency occurred.

And here I must digress to describe what I remember about Dr. Cressy, one of the great personalities of Wallington at that time. He was tall and very handsome, and always dressed in a frock-coat, complete with grey top hat; white gloves; and a monocle. He and his charming wife, a pretty lady but rarely seen, lived in a secluded large house at the bottom of Manor Road where it joins Croydon Road, surrounded by high brick walls. The surgery was not a very comfortable place, furnished mainly with hard wooden benches, with the consulting-room leading off. Most medicines would be made up by the doctor on the spot, with assorted colours and flavourings added, then duly corked and labelled in small or large bottles. I don't recall any written records being kept, but of course notes may have been made after the surgery closed.

It was a great honour to be invited into Mrs. Cressy's drawing-room for some special reason, and I remember it as being full of flowers and chintz covers. There was always an air of secret tragedy to be felt, as their only son had died in sad circumstances (whether through the Great War or an illness I am not sure, but think it was the former).

Dr. Cressy used to drive around to make his calls in an open carriage for many years, and would enter the house at speed, fling his hat and gloves on the hall table, and sweep upstairs to inspect the patient. Woe betide anyone who dared to argue or question his verdict and instructions; and even my father (who feared nothing on earth and later went out quite happily to the warden's post during air raids) would be cowed by the doctor's presence. My

1

mother had several spells of illness over many years and had complete faith in Dr. Cressy to pull her through. He certainly steered her through an illness following the birth of my younger sister, which brought her close to death, and visited the house night and morning for weeks, putting the fear of God into the nurse who was caring for her and forbidding my father to mow the lawn in case the noise disturbed Mother!

Later on, the horse and carriage gave way to a chauffeur-driven limousine, and the whole town mourned when the legendary doctor eventually died. He was instrumental, with others in founding the War Memorial Hospital at Carshalton, I believe, and for some years he attended at the private nursing-home in Woodcote Road, Wallington (near the site of the present Town Hall) where minor operations were carried out.

My father did not qualify for what was then known as being 'on the panel', so all medical and dental fees had to be paid by him — quite an undertaking for a man with a wife and family.

By way of a postcript to my memories of the doctor, I have never forgotten the proud moment when he arrived just as I was carrying up a tray to Mother (we were without help at the time and I had to stay away from school to look after her during an illness), and he said, 'If you can make a rice pudding as good as that, you're all right.'

I was the first-born and my parents were at that time living in Waddon Court Road on the outskirts of Croydon, but it seems that my mother very soon suffered from loneliness and disliked the separation from her own family, so she badgered my father until he agreed to return to Wallington and they then set up house in what was known as 'The Myrtles' in Park Lane, only a few minutes away from my grandparents and various aunts and uncles.

By this time I was about two or three years old, and of course the next phase in my life was greatly influenced by changes caused by the outbreak of the First World War in 1914. My father joined the Army, having previously belonged to the Surrey Yeomanry; mother let the house furnished; and we went back to live with my grandparents for the duration at 'Normanhurst' in Grosvenor Road, the large detached family residence which, in addition to possessing several bedrooms, a morning-room, a gun-room and coach-house, was blessed with huge cellars and walk-in pantries under the house, thus providing very secure shelters from possible air-raids. In fact I can still recall spending several nights down there during the Zeppelin attacks on London and thought it great fun, not realising the potential dangers, of course. In normal times the shelves of these pantries were crammed with milk, eggs and butter (for coolness), cold roast joints, bowls of stewed fruit, and so on. The other part of the cellarage housed bottles of wine; coal, wood and garden brooms, etc.

From this distance I see now that the Wallington of my own childhood was still largely the village that my mother had known in her young days, as compared with the large outer London suburb that it has since become. However, this was not quite the historic Hamlet of Wallington. This Walling-

2

*Manor Road (1903) looking north. On the left is the north end of Railway Terrace;
on the right is the Melbourne Public House; and in the far distance the spire of
Holy Trinity Church. The entrance to Grosvenor Road can be seen just
beyond the lamp-post on the left.*

*Normanhurst (formerly number 2) Grosvenor Road.
The home of John Charles Albert Forsdick, the author's grandfather.*
Photograph by Frank Burgess, 1979

ton was now centred round the station on what had been fields before the second half of the 19th century — the old village, or hamlet, was now on the fringe of Wallington, by the Green — and was itself a nineteenth century suburban growth.

The mental picture of the place as remembered by Mother and so often recounted to me reveals a green in Melbourne Road (the site of the former Post Office) where she tethered her pony and pet donkey on land owned by her father; and chalky banks near the newly-built railway where she and her brothers often slid down in their Sunday-best and were severely punished for such escapades! Another childish prank was to empty the Council's water-cart which was stored in Forsdick's yard during the week-end, so that the driver had to refill it on a Monday morning, much to their secret delight: not very laudable, but true. John Forsdick, her father, combined various farming activities with his local contractor's business of sixty horses, a black-smith's forge and (later) luxurious hired cars and garages on the land now in use as a car park adjoining the railway station. Lavender fields and acres of peppermint were grown by him where the smallholdings now flourish at the top of Boundary Road, and Mother would often be taken for picnic teas in these scented fields as a young child. The harvest of lavender flowers was regularly distilled by Miss Sprules at her still in Melbourne Road, and was used in the famous Mitcham Lavender toilet products for many years.

Mother's early days were spent at their first family residence, known as 'Sunnydale', a farmhouse-type dwelling in the area known as Forsdick's Yard, close to the station and reached through a tiny wicket-gate. The horses were stabled there, and I can remember lots of chickens and various other domestic animals and pets always underfoot, as I often visited my grand-father while he was in his office there, after they had removed to the Grosvenor Road house.

The local fire engine was also housed in the Yard, and was maintained by Dick Chandler who was the caretaker at the old Council offices in Belmont Road (now the site of the modern fire station).

Horses owned by my grandfather were used to pull the engine before the days of mechanisation.

In the centre of the village the local tradesmen were important and pros-perous, and known to everyone; and it was quite usual for carriages to bring 'the gentry' to shop in person, and to see nursemaids wheeling out their charges in the afternoons. Many of these shopkeepers were interesting per-sonalities and I have described them in a separate chapter all to themselves, as I feel they deserve their place in history as being part of a breed no longer in existence in these days of impersonal self-service and supermarkets.

*Harvesting lavender in the fields around Wallington at the turn of the century.*

*A water van, possibly the one referred to in Chapter One. The photograph is believed to have been taken in the 1890s outside Dr. Cressy's house at the corner of Manor Road and Croydon Road, opposite Wallington Green.*

*The author's grandmother,*
*Harriet Forsdick*

*John Charles Albert Forsdick,*
*the author's grandfather*

# CHAPTER TWO

## *Grandparents, Aunts and Uncles*

Regarding my grandparents, these have of course become rather shadowy figures to me now, but I remember hearing that my maternal grandmother, Harriet Forsdick, was spoken of as a very beautiful woman, and I do recall that she was tall and amply-built. She was also very domesticated, and a real mother-figure to her six children and ten grandchildren as she competently presided over the large house and garden at Normanhurst, with the aid of one of those good old-fashioned living-in maids, Lotty, together with a washerwoman and the occasional gardener to help with the heavy digging and planting. The one I liked best was known as 'Old Goody' and stayed with the family business as odd-job man all his working life. With so many horses there was always plenty of manure to be spread around the kitchen garden to enrich the soil and produce super vegetables!

Grandmother seldom went out, as most of the provisions were ordered and delivered to the house regularly; but she seemed to have a full and happy life with her cooking, jam-making, sewing and general supervising. In the evenings she would sometimes play the piano in the drawing-room and sing one of the currently popular songs – her favourites being from 'The Student Prince'. The flowers she liked best were lilies-of-the-valley and there was an enormous bed of these in a shady corner of the garden, drenching the air with their special fragrance. I often used to go round for tea with Granny and was very fond of her. As a special privilege I would sometimes be allowed to go upstairs with her after dinner and stay while she changed for the afternoon. I can still picture her applying Pond's vanishing cream and a lotion, sweetly scented and named 'Larola', to her face and neck, as she took a great pride in her complexion and general appearance. She was, in fact, almost the first lady in Wallington to have her hair cut, tinted and permanently waved – a great revolutionary step at that time. She was also very fond of jewellery; and made a great fuss of her pet dog, a Pomeranian named Doody, which was always given a saucer of tea when we sat at table for that meal.

Occasionally both grandparents would dress up to the hilt, he with waxed moustache and smelling slightly of Eau-de-Cologne, for a visit to the Grand Theatre in Croydon, or for supper at the Café Royal in the High Street there, where shaded pink lamps lit the tables, and waiters in evening dress added lustre to birthday treats.

Grandmother's death at the age of only sixty-three, following a coronary thrombosis which resulted in her lying in a coma for three months, left a gap in the family which was never filled. She was buried in Bandon Hill Cemetery (where her husband was later buried too) and apparently Mother was led sobbing from the graveside. She never really ceased to grieve for the loss of her parents to whom she was deeply devoted.

John Charles Albert Forsdick was born in London but went with his family as a boy to live in Banstead, where his father became the licensee of the Old Tangiers Inn (afterwards burnt down and never replaced), also the occupant of the adjoining farm. Grandfather went for a few years after leaving school — the Dame School housed in an old stone dwelling in Woodmansterne Lane — to work in his uncle's timber business, Messrs. Joshua Knight's, in London. He then returned to his father's business which had by this time moved to Wallington.

He might have become a steeplechase jockey, for he was a brilliant rider and rode in the trials at Epsom; and in later years he was a keen rider to hounds, possessing some very good hunters. He hunted with the Old Surrey Fox Hounds and the West Surrey Stag Hounds, but never allowed sport to interfere with his business which for over fifty years he built up until his name was known all over Surrey. He was also a well-known Mason, being the oldest member of the Croydon Lodge of Concord (No.463).

Grandfather was essentially a man who lived entirely for his family and the business, seldom taking a holiday and constantly worrying over the state of the country generally, or the misdeeds of his sons in particular. He was a dedicated gardener, and as a child I was quite frightened of picking anything at Normanhurst without permission. He always warned me only to 'pick the old mint, never the young shoots' — a maxim I still bear in mind!

That particular garden in Grosvenor Road possessed a number of rather special features, including a huge walnut tree; a large raised-up fish-pond full of water-lilies and goldfish; an ancient asparagus bed most carefully nurtured; and two long greenhouses full of peaches, nectarines, grapes and tomatoes — all in a lovely steamy hot atmosphere! It was a rare treat to be cut a tiny bunch of grapes, or given a juicy fragrant peach; and I still recall my grandfather telling me the old fable about the fox and the grapes. All over the inside roofs of the greenhouses there trailed the most lovely scented pure white rose that I have ever seen, and have never found the equal since, though I have searched through many a garden catalogue.

There was also a large tennis-lawn at the side of the house, edged with pergolas of rambling roses leading up to a spacious wooden summer-house where we sometimes had tea. At the far end of the vast kitchen garden there

*The Grand Theatre*
*South End, Croydon*

*Coach trip from Bognor Regis. The author's parents, Henry and Maude Lawrence*
*(née Forsdick) seated, second row from the front. Behind, Waterloo Square. The*
*picture shows sheep grazing on the grass enclosure.*

*Wedding group in the back garden of Normanhurst. In the centre are Henry Charles Lawrence and his bride (née Maude Forsdick)*

was a cosy potting-shed and a very old apple-tree whose beautiful gnarled branches were garlanded with misletoe — an unusual occurrence which has remained in my memory ever since.

The conservatory which led out of the morning-room at the back of the house was another place which I recall with great pleasure as it was always filled by my grandfather with a fascinating selection of ferns and indoor plants of many kinds, and we children were often given the task of keeping them all watered.

Mother was married from Normanhurst in mid-July of 1909, on a day of brilliant sunshine judging from the splendid summer gowns and enormous shady hats of the guests. The garden was a riot of roses and sweet peas, and it seems that the whole village gathered together in the parish church in Manor Road and later at the reception at Normanhurst, since people still spoke about that great day many years later and described champagne flowing like water for all present! I recently came across the silver-printed Menu set out for the guests in a marquee in the garden, so I print it here just as it was, all in French, for the record:-

Filets de Saumon en Mayonnaise
Concombre
Cailles à la Lucullus
Côtelettes d'Agneau à la Duchesse
Poulets Rôtis  Jambon d'York
Canetons Rôtis  Paté de Pigeon
Langue de Boeuf
Salade Coeur de Laitues
. . . . .
Pêches Melba
Crème de Fraises
Chartreuse de Bananes
Meringues à la Crème
Glaces Venitienne
Dessert  Café

The bridegroom, Henry Charles Lawrence from Croydon, was considered to be the most handsome bachelor in the neighbourhood, and they certainly made a splendid pair in the wedding photographs. Sadly, however, the promise of happiness did not materialise; but that is another story.

Looking at these photographs reminds me that the Forsdick family was quite large by today's standards, since Mother had three brothers and two sisters: known to me in due course as Uncle Bert, Uncle Ben, Uncle Cecil, Aunt Marjorie and Aunt Renée. Completing the wider family was their father's brother and his wife, known as Old Uncle Ben and Aunt Polly, who lived in a small cottage in Clifton Road, Wallington (he being rather an eccentric person not keen on work and largely supported by the rest of the family financially).

Their tiny garden was edged with a privet hedge and filled with old-fashioned cottage flowers such as velvety pansies, sweetscented mignonette and the white 'Mrs. Sinkins' pinks; and I always enjoyed a visit there for tea, as Aunt Polly was a very gentle motherly soul (though they had no children) and made delectable preserves, especially her marrow-ginger jam which I have never been able to equal!

Old Uncle Ben was, I am sorry to say, a fanatic about horses and hunting, and as children we always used to run away if we saw him coming down the road as he had a most disconcerting habit of standing stock-still and crying out in a loud voice 'Tally-ho', then reciting 'Do ye ken John Peel'! He did this to the end of his days, and always wore a Billy-cock hard hat to complete the picture.

The three other uncles I have mentioned were all educated at both Wallington High School for Boys and Whitgift Grammar School at Croydon, but although Uncle Bert and Uncle Ben, on returning from war service in the Middle East, both joined the family business, they proved endlessly disappointing to their father, Ben preferring to spend his time at Epsom races or in the nearby public-house known as 'The Melbourne', where, with his handsome Alsatian dog, Rex, he became a well-known personality until he died.

Uncle Cecil, who delighted me as a child with his great sense of fun and humour, in due course joined the Merchant Navy and later had a very successful career in the oil industry. Together with his wife and two children he lived in Wallington for the remainder of his life.

My two aunts were typical 'flappers' of those early days, tying their long hair back with huge stiff black ribbon bows. Aunt Marjorie was considered quite adventurous when she went daily to London to work at 'The Bank' and she was later a bride of the First World War years. In due course she and her husband with their four children took up residence in Grosvenor Road almost opposite Normanhurst, so that I often was able to go to tea with my cousins and we largely grew up together.

Aunt Renée was also a great favourite of mine, as she was a real fashion-plate and I loved to be allowed to spend time up in her bedroom while she was dressing to go to a dance or out to dinner with one of her many admirers. Crêpe-de-chine and georgette lace-edged petticoats and cami-knickers in a gorgeous array of colours and designs would lay scattered about the room, and I would totter round in her high-heeled silver evening slippers while she arranged her hair and pinned on the corsage of roses or carnations sent from the florists by her escort. Sometimes it might even be an orchid, and this would be carefully placed in a tiny vase on her dressing-table when she returned in the early hours.

After the death of my grandmother this same aunt took over the housekeeping and looked after her father until his death; but she also managed to spend several exciting holidays in France and made many friends.

*Great Aunt Polly Forsdick*

*The author's Aunt Renée and Uncle Cecil as children*

*The Forsdick family outside Normanhurst. From left to right: Maude (the eldest), Bert, Renée, John and Harriet Forsdick (the author's grandparents), Cecil (in front) with Marjorie, and Ben standing behind her.*

13

*Maude Forsdick,
the author's mother,
as a child.*

*Maude Forsdick
(seated left on floor)
with her parents, and
her two brothers, Bert,
and Ben (the baby).*

14

# CHAPTER THREE

## Parents and Sisters

When I come to put down what I remember about my parents I come up against the most difficult barriers of all, since my childhood judgment and loyalties were (unwittingly) clouded and prejudiced by the never-ending quarrels that flared as the result of the love-hate relationship between them, inevitably involving my sisters and me. Basically they were incompatible, and Mother, having been brought up in an indulgent and extravagant atmosphere, continually expected my father to provide her with more housekeeping money than he could reasonably afford. In those days women were always 'kept in the dark' as to their husband's earnings, so they never really knew whether they were getting a fair share. How much better it is now that things are more open in most marriages, where the family income and budget are freely discussed by both partners.

Many years later, when I had been married and lived in my own home for some long time, I was able to stand back, as it were, and see more clearly both sides of their sad problem, and thus to reassess and revise the emotional and immature judgments of my childhood. One aspect in particular has since struck me as very odd: despite the almost daily occurrence of bitter quarrels and hysterical scenes in our household, I can find no trace *whatsoever* of these miseries in any of my personal diaries which I began to keep at about the age of ten and have continued throughout my life. I can only assume that they were so much part and parcel of our daily life that it was not worth mentioning them, since they came into the same category as getting up, having meals, going to bed and so on (although I see that I did include daily mention of such things as the weather, what I did in my leisure time, the friends I met, family illnesses, and so on). Modern psychiatrists might have something to say on this subject, with their emphasis on the effect of unhappy homes and marriages. The one thing I do recall is being somewhat afraid to get married myself in case it all turned out for the worse. In those days divorce was almost unheard of, and, as most women did not have any training for a career they could not risk giving up their homes, as

15

*En route to Ascot Races, c. 1908. Maude Forsdick, the author's mother, seated at the front of the horse-brake, in a frilly hat; and her father, next but one to the driver. On the far left, Mr. Millest, the grocer whose shop was in the Station Approach, Wallington.*

16

it was financially impossible to support themselves and their children except in the poorest circumstances. Things now seem to have gone to the other extreme, when, at the drop of a hat, marriages are broken up and no one need put up with years of unhappiness. Either way it is the children who are the main victims.

Returning to my mother; Maude Mary Ann, as she was christened, was temperamental, vivacious and thoroughly spoilt by the family from the start, she being the eldest and possessing a strong personality. At the age of about six she was sent off to the little Dame School run by Miss Bonwick in Bridge Road, and excelled herself by spending the shilling given her for the week's fee on buying a flaxen-haired doll she had long admired in the toy shop in Manor Road! Returning home proudly with this she was amazed when Grandmother (her mother) took it away and chastised her. Old Grandfather Forsdick came upon her screaming on the stone kitchen floor and eventually insisted that she be given back the doll. No wonder that she grew up spoilt! This episode was used to tease Mother at that shop for many years.

Her next school was, I believe, known as the Wallington High School for the Daughters of Gentlefolk, and was situated at the junction of Manor Road and Queen's Road. This later became the Wallington County School for Girls where we children followed in her footsteps and had the same teacher in Form 1 — dear Mrs. Newton, a war widow who had been obliged to return to her teaching career to keep herself and her two children. The discipline in Mother's day was quite fantastically strict, with no speaking whatsoever allowed in the class and the severe headmistress liable to burst into the room at any moment and administer punishment to wrong-doers.

On Saturday mornings Mother used to ride in the pony and trap with her father, along the rough lane which is now Stafford Road, to collect the weekly provisions from the large grocers in North End, Croydon. I think the name was Williamsons. In winter her hands became frozen, she would tell us, despite being wrapped up in rugs, and Grandfather would give her a sip of the mid-morning port which he always indulged in at the public-house before the return journey.

When she was in her 'teens, Mother would often drive her friends out in the little pony-trap on summer evenings, trotting round the quiet Surrey lanes or occasionally pulling up to gather primroses and bluebells. Her special and life-long friend was Rose Stafford (later to become the well-known and loved Mrs. Sid Miller of Mitcham Junction, where the Millers grew their famous water-cress and built up a flourishing market-garden business for many years).

As soon as schooldays were over my mother and her friends made the most of the limited range of entertainments available and took part in quite a pleasant round of social events such as musical evenings in each other's homes, charity concerts, private dances, and trips on the River Thames or to the races. My mother had a beautiful soprano voice and took regular singing lessons, and this made her much in demand to sing at charity concerts. At one of these she was accompanied on the piano by the famous

*The author's parents, grandparents and friends, on a boat trip down the river c. 1908*

composer, Samuel Coleridge Taylor, who lived in the district and is buried in Bandon Hill cemetery. I think she was all her life a frustrated woman who should have taken up a professional singing career and not become tied within the limitations of marriage and motherhood.

The river trips mentioned above were organised by John Forsdick who provided the horses and carriages; and after Mother's death, when I had to sort out her personal papers, I found a menu dated June, 1908, which she had kept from one of these outings; and it certainly makes memorable reading since it includes items as follows:-

**On Arrival:** Sandwiches and Meat Patties.
Biscuits and Cheese.

**Luncheon:** Salmon Mayonnaise, Roast Chicken, York Ham.
Veal and Ham Pie, Pigeon Pie, Salads.
Strawberry Cream or Pineapple Cream.
Fruit Tarts.

Ices to be served during the afternoon.

**Tea at 5.30:** Prawn Sandwiches.
White and Brown Bread and Butter.
Cherry and Madeira Cakes.
Fancy Cakes, Preserves.
Strawberries, Watercress, etc.
Tea and Coffee.

Wines, Spirits and Cigars also obtainable as desired.

I may add as a footnote that my parents and most of my relatives have lived into their eighties or nineties with hardly an operation or serious illness between them, so the menus of their day do not seem to have shortened their lives!.

Visits to the dressmakers and milliners took up quite a large portion of those days, since they involved several fittings and much purchasing of materials and choosing of patterns for each creation. Of course, as the family grew larger, Mother was expected to help with the care of the younger children, but all in all she seems to have had quite a good life, and, indeed, she constantly told us in later years that those days were the happiest she could remember.

The first appearance of my father in her life was, I believe, at one of the dances arranged by 'The Bohemians' at Croydon, where he was the M.C. (Master of Ceremonies for the programme). It was inevitable that they should be attracted to each other visually, she being very pretty and petite and he being handsome and somewhat more mature than her other friends as he was six years older than she. His home life had been somewhat disastrous owing to the fact that his father had drunk or gambled away the family inheritance and died before Mother married Father. His mother, Emily, was

*The author's father, Henry Charles Lawrence, in the uniform of the Surrey Yeomanry*

a gentle soul and a great beauty, but sadly she too died in early middle-age so I never knew her.

My main memories of Father are that he was utterly undomesticated; that he lived for his life as a successful businessman in the City of London, where he was eventually managing director of his firm (D. A. Fyffe & Co., forage merchants of Eldon St., E.C.1) and regularly attended at the Corn Exchange; and that he refused to consider retirement until he was over seventy and had suffered two strokes. He was a great fighter in the mental sense and re-covered his health sufficiently to be able to continue going to his office on a twice-weekly basis to advise for several more years.

I have inherited my great love of animals from my father, who insisted that the household should always include a dog, a cat and a canary — a rather tricky situation, but I never remember any disasters arising from the trio. We also had regular visits from hedgehogs in the garden and my father often put out saucers of milk for them very late at night.

Another personal pleasure of Father's was his clothes, as he prided himself on never wearing the same suit or pair of shoes two days running! When plus-fours were introduced he was among the first to wear them at week-ends; and used to spend ages in the bathroom at night and in the morning, grooming his hair and bathing, etc., thus delaying the rest of the family! He did not smoke cigarettes often but loved his pipe, and one of my treasures today is the heavy brown and green earthenware bowl which still retains a faint fragrance from the tobacco which he always kept in it; thanks to the massive lid and quaint metal fastener.

A great treat for me was my occasional visit to Father's London office on a Saturday morning, where the clerks and secretaries would be requested to keep me amused with paper and pencils, plus a spare typewriter which I could pretend to use until it was time for us to go out to lunch in Father's regular restaurant. Quite often he would take me in the afternoon to a performance at the Victoria Palace or the Coliseum, where famous variety stars of the day were appearing. We would also visit our local cinemas in Sutton or Croydon on Saturday evenings, where such favourites as Douglas Fairbanks and Mary Pickford could be seen. Father was a great lover of films, but Mother hated them, so I think he was pleased to take me with him for company and relaxation at the week-ends. But we *always* and unfailingly had to bring back some sweets as compensation for Mother — usually the very expensive and mouth-watering candies from Fuller's in Croydon or Sutton. They have long since disappeared but have never been equalled for sheer quality and variety. You could make your own selection in the shop and they were then put with silver tongs into a white carton, scarlet-lettered and drawn up with cord.

Father always insisted on high standards in the personal cleanliness and behaviour of us children. He was 'very faddy' (to quote Mother) regarding his food, but was very fond of sweets and always kept a fancy tin filled with delicious jellies, fondants, peppermint creams and all kinds of candies which

*The author (standing on the chair) with her mother and baby sister, Joan*

we children were allowed to sample only on invitation, since we each had our own weekly pocket-money to spend on ourselves for such delights. He was not remotely interested in art, books or music — though he was a choir-boy at Croydon Parish Church when young — and I must confess that I have still no real knowledge of his inner emotions or approach to life, as he always prided himself on 'keeping a stiff upper lip'. As children my sisters and I were forced by Mother to take sides against him, so my views were prejudiced; but in London, among his business associates, he was known as 'The Man with the Smile', so I feel he must have been quite a popular figure. He also achieved high office in his Masonic life, which was a great source of pleasure and pride to him. After his retirement he moved to Sussex and lies now in a quiet churchyard, together with Mother — in peace at last.

Completing this chapter on my immediate family, I now come to describe my two sisters, Joan and Peggy, but as they are both at the time of writing still very much alive I shall have to bear this in mind!

Joan was born in the middle of the First World War and turned out to be the artist in the family, following this career in a London studio until she married and later moved to live in the country. I hesitate to refer again to personal beauty in the family but Mother often recalled how people praised her three babies for their looks, for in those days plump children with curly hair were greatly admired and it was a disgrace to have any bones showing through one's flesh!

Peggy, of the sky-blue eyes and flaxen curls, was born a few years later, after our return to The Myrtles when the war was over. She was forever full of gaiety and laughter, and collected plenty of admirers before she, in turn, married, and moved away to live in the Provinces for some years until she and her husband returned to the South.

We all went in due course to the same school in Wallington, and at one period were all there together. We each had our own set of friends, and very different personalities, but the common thread of having to endure the parental unhappiness at home became a bond which has survived more than a few crises of family life.

Carshalton Park, quite close to The Myrtles, was our favourite play-ground apart from the garden at home, and we all spent many happy hours there, racing up and down the grassy hillocks, or fishing for tiddlers and tadpoles along the river banks where the glorious chestnut trees swept down to the water's edge, and close to the famous Grotto where we loved to play hide-and-seek. Later on we used to cycle down to The Grove in Carshalton and enjoy the picturesque grounds there.

Probably the most important mutual interest we three have had, however, is an abiding passion for the countryside and the sea — borne out by the fact that we all now live within ten miles of each other in the sunshine and peace of the West Sussex coast.

23

*The Myrtles, 38 Park Lane, the author's childhood home.*
Photograph by Frank Burgess, 1979.

# CHAPTER FOUR

## Home Life

Looking back I realise that we were unashamedly members of the comfortable middle-class, living at The Myrtles in Park Lane, which was a detached house (covered by rosy Virginia creeper) with four bedrooms, front and back hall, drawing-room, dining-room, kitchen, scullery, bathroom, etc., plus a conservatory, aviary, tool-shed, and outside lavatory for the gardener or visiting workmen. The front garden was edged by privet hedges, with gravelled path and flower beds, and the back was largely lawn with fruit trees and a rockery. Father hated gardening, so periodically Grandfather would arrive together with 'Old Goody' and between them they would carry out some piece of improvement to please Mother. We also had a grand swing under the rose-covered pergolas.

Our neighbours consisted of elderly couples on both sides, whom we had to be very careful not to annoy by playing noisy games or throwing balls over the fence. When this did happen, I would have to go and knock at Mrs. Slade's front door and request permission to retrieve the ball. She was a very pleasant lady, with no children of her own, and would often invite me to have a glass of home-made barley-water with a slice of Madeira cake before returning home! Those were the days when people took great pride in 'keeping themselves to themselves' and I cannot remember a single occasion when Mother entered either house for a social event such as taking tea, though she remained on good terms with the neighbours throughout the forty years she lived at The Myrtles. Incidentally, the couple who later bought the next-door house after Mr. Slade's death turned out to be none other than the well-known broadcaster and traveller, Commander Campbell, and his wife.

Our front door was notable for its very fine stained-glass panels, and of course in those days there were cream lace curtains and green Venetian blinds at the windows — later to be replaced by more modern chintz hangings, as the interiors were redecorated in white paint instead of the boring old brown. In the hall, on the leather-topped table, stood our black tele-

*Jenny, a maid in the household at The Myrtles, seen here with the family dog, 'Duke'*

phone, one of the first in the district; and from my earliest days I can remember being trained to answer it correctly and politely, as it was quite rare to be 'on the 'phone' then. Coal fires were lit throughout the winter in the dining-room and kitchen, and also in the drawing-room at week-ends; but of course there were no such extra comforts as gas-fires or electric fires for the chilly spring or summer evenings. Probably the extra clothes we all wore helped to keep us warm enough, as I do not recall ever worrying about the cold. We were, however, very glad to take advantage of the growing fashion for woollen pullovers and cardigans to be worn by both sexes — hitherto mainly only schoolboys wore jerseys as additions to their grey flannel suits, while older men wore waistcoats. Stone hot-water bottles and bedsocks were relied upon to keep one warm on frosty nights!

Housework at that time was quite hard, in the absence of modern vacuum cleaners and electric polishers, since all floors had to be kept clean by 'carpet-sweepers' or by throwing used tea-leaves on the floor and sweeping these up with long stiff brooms. Every room had to be 'turned out' once a week, involving great moving of chairs and furniture. In our drawing-room this was further complicated by Mother's enormous collection of Goss china and miniatures of all kinds, kept in the glass-fronted cabinet and only to be dusted by her. In actual fact they were so minute that she could, I suspect, only blow on them and dare not risk picking many of them up!

We always had a maid 'living in', plus a little elderly widow, Mrs. Nichols from Hackbridge, who arrived by bus every Monday morning to help with the washing, although of course all the bed-linen was sent to the laundry. There was a large copper (a circular metal container, set in a brick structure, under which a small fire burned to heat the water) out in the scullery where most of the washing would be done, in a hot steamy atmosphere, especially on a wet day when the doors and window had to be kept shut. After drying the washing out on the line in the garden, the rest of the day and evening would be spent on the ironing, and the garments would then be folded and arranged on the wooden airing-rack which was pulled up to the kitchen ceiling over the heat from the fire. Heavy items would also have been put through the iron mangle, which stood out in the garden shed and involved a nasty cold job on wintry days. I should also add that the ironing had to be done by two flat-irons which were heated on the kitchen range or gas cooker. It all seems very far away from these days of drip-dry materials, washing-machines and spin-dryers!

On the subject of maids, names of those I can remember include Martha, Blanche and Jenny — our dear and faithful Jenny who stayed for twenty years and waited hand and foot on Mother during her many illnesses. She came from a very large and poor family in Norfolk and had been sent away to a mansion in Eaton Square, London, to train as a housemaid. During this period, however, she fell from grace by 'getting into trouble' with a police-man. After being dismissed and having the baby in some kind of charitable institution she came to us as a general maid, but her disgrace was kept secret for twenty years and we children never had the slightest suspicion that Jenny had in fact a daughter of her own who was being brought up by the grandmother in far-away Norfolk.

Many were the tales Jenny told us of high life in the London of those days when she was in service with a titled family. On evenings when our parents had gone to the theatre in London, or out to supper with friends, Jenny would play dressing-up games with us, when we became Lords and Ladies giving dinner-parties, complete with finger-bowls and wineglasses! She was a fantastically hard worker and would polish our hall floor with what she called 'elbow grease' until it was a positive danger to walk across, in case the rugs slipped; much to my father's annoyance.

Another maid I remember was Martha, who excelled herself by being discovered to be a 'carrier' of the dreaded (in those days) diphtheria and passing it on to the three of us children. In those days of mainly long hair it was often a tussle to ensure that the maid washed her hair regularly and kept herself clean and tidy. They all, of course, wore uniforms − plain blue or mauve dresses with long white aprons and caps in the mornings; brown or green dresses with frilly aprons and dainty caps to match in the afternoons. In our house, the little front bedroom over the porch was always the maid's room, complete with her trunk and personal belongings, and was forbidden territory to us unless invited in. The kitchen was where she sat in the evenings after all the washing-up and ironing was done.

We possessed a set of old-fashioned bells in the house and my father thought it quite normal to ring the bell through to the kitchen for the maid to 'bring another plate' or 'make up the fire'. The usual practice was for the maid to have one half-day per week off, also every other Sunday afternoon and evening (which we hated because we had to get the tea and supper and do the washing-up!). I suppose she went to the local cinema or did any personal shopping or visited a nearby friend, but she must always be back promptly by 10.30 p.m. She also came away with us to stay in our boarding-house or hotel when the summer holidays came round every July. This, of course, enabled our parents to go off and enjoy their evenings with a clear conscience, knowing that the children were being looked after, although it was not called baby-sitting at that time.

Very often my parents' outing would be 'up to town' (i.e. to London's West End—we never called it London, but always just 'town') to see such legendary musical comedies as Chu-Chin-Chow; The Maid of the Mountains (starring the famous José Collins); and later Rose Marie, The Desert Song, The Vagabond King and so on. These lavish productsion and the matinée idols who acted in them were regular topics of conversation; as frequent late trains ran from Victoria Station to all the suburbs − much later in fact than at present − so outings to London for theatres or dinners at, for instance, the famous Trocadero were easily undertaken without benefit of cars.

Mother bought all the music of the shows to play and sing to on her prized rosewood piano, and I can remember crying quietly to myself in a corner

*Manor Road and Station Approach, Wallington, c. 1900. King's, the florist, can be seen (centre) and the Melbourne Public House (far left). The last shop in Railway Terrace (right) is French and Co., the photographers, and next to this, just out of sight in the Station Approach, is the entrance to Forsdick's Yard and, beyond that, Millest's the grocers.*

*Woodcote Road, Wallington, c. 1935, at the junction of Ross Parade (left) showing the semi-circular canopy of the Odeon Cinema, and Tilley and Aldis (drapers) now the Post Office.*

of the sofa while she sang in her high soprano voice many of the sentimental ballads of the day, such as 'Parted', 'The Rosary', 'The Sunshine of your Smile', the 'Indian Love Lyrics' and many more.

Compared with modern days, Mother obviously had a pretty easy time as far as household running was concerned, since it was the custom for practically everything to be delivered, if one wished, by errand boy on bicycle or by van. Twice a week one of the grocer's assistants from Millest's in Railway Approach would call at the house in the morning and be admitted to the kitchen, where he would sit down and write in his order book a list of our grocery requirements — which would be delivered later that day. The butcher and fishmonger also sent daily orders, and of course bread came every day. Fresh vegetables and fruit could be bought regularly from nearby small-holdings along Woodmansterne Lane whose owners called in a van; while, as for milk and cream — the first delivery was at 6 a.m., to be followed by another about noon! The milk was in a huge metal churn and was ladled by hand into one's own small churn or jug. I believe we had about three deliveries of post every weekday, and certainly numerous collections.

My mother also had a weakness for new hats and would think nothing of telephoning the local draper's shop (Aldis and Hutchings, later Tilley and Aldis, in Woodcote Road, now the site of the Post Office) and asking for a selection of hats to be sent round on approval — and if this desire happened to come over her around five o'clock, sure enough the little old delivery man would stagger round later on that same evening, complete with hat-box crammed full, because it was quite usual for most shops to remain open until seven or eight, or even later. For too many it was the bad old days.

Although I was in due course presented with two sisters; looking back I realise that Mother's pregnancies were completely hidden from me, and indeed from most of the neighbourhood. I seem to remember that she suddenly took to going out mostly after dark for her daily walk, wearing a long navy-blue cloak; and later, when a resident trained nurse arrived, she was simply introduced as a friend who was staying with us for a few weeks. I may have glimpsed a beautiful baby basket of wicker, lace-frilled and threaded with narrow baby ribbon, being gradually filled with tiny brush and comb, swansdown puff and baby powder, cotton-wool and so on; also the white swinging cot was freshly painted and re-hung with dotted muslin and ribbon bows. But no one thought it necessary or desirable to prepare us in any way for the sudden arrival of a new baby, and one just accepted the fact that it appeared 'out of the blue' or 'from under the gooseberry bushes', so any thoughts of jealousy or being deprived of attention never entered one's head, as far as I can recall. Most babies were, of course, born at home, so there was plenty of excitement at all the strange activities, and pride in being allowed to help push the grand new pram on its first outing. Actually one of my very first memories must have been of one of these occasions, since I clearly remember going down to Carshalton, with the maid pushing my sister in her pram, in order that I might feed the ducks in the famous ponds. Incidentally, that is where I first met my friend, Henry Haydon, of similar age, whose family had occupied 'The Banks' and butchers' business in Carshalton High Street for nearly three hundred years until the buildings were destroyed during the Second World War. He and I later became committee members of the Junior Municipal League in the district and the Wallington House of Commons; and later still he was to become the last Mayor of the former Borough of Beddington and Wallington.

This description of general home life would be incomplete without a few memories of meals, for Mother was an excellent cook and had been brought up in a family which only bought the best quality of everything. Breakfast cereals had not been invented, so we had always the usual bacon and eggs or tomatoes, or poached eggs, or kippers, or (on Sundays) cold small pork sausages, with, of course, toast and marmalade to follow. 'Elevenses' as such were not usual, though grown-ups often had a glass of burgundy or sherry, and at one o'clock, unfailingly, we all came home from school (except a very few who lived at Sutton and were entitled to hot or cold lunch) and sat down to a hot dinner. This might be steak-and-kidney pie or pudding, lamb chops, veal cutlets, steak casserole, steak and onions, Irish stew, or plaice or Dover soles (cod and herrings and such-like were despised by us as being 'common'!). All meat courses were accompanied by some form of potatoes and fresh vegetables, generally two kinds, according to season. A hot pudding would follow, such as steamed sultana pudding or syrup sponge, fruit tart, or rice pudding, and so on, ringing the changes on the well-known English recipes of the time. On Sundays, of course, it was invariably a roast joint of some kind — beef, pork or lamb in turn, with all the trimmings of horseradish sauce, apple sauce and mint sauce (all fresh) respectively. Turkey and chicken were regarded as great treats and normally only appeared on Christmas Day — somewhat different from the present time when they are commonplace items on menus. The Sunday pudding course was always rather special, though, and might consist of a trifle or fruit jelly, or stewed prunes with blancmange; but in every case we in our house always had fresh cream added, plus delicious peeled almonds. The mind boggles at the thought of it all now, as well as the cost!

After school finished at about 4 o'clock, we would return home on our bicycles, and at five we would sit down to a proper afternoon tea, with white and brown bread-and-butter, and jam or paste, plus a great variety of cakes. Quite often Mother would instruct me to 'pop down to Miss Brown the baker's' in Manor Road and fetch a shillings-worth of fancies — that is, about twelve or thirteen of the most delectable small iced cakes in various shapes and flavours; or, as an alternative, we often indulged in some of the tiny pink or white meringues from Riddington's in Woodcote Road, with cream from Short's Dairy close by. Needless to say, after such meals all we children were given was a very light bed-time snack of biscuits and milk or home-made lemonade (or cocoa in winter); but the grown-ups of course later sat down to supper or 'late dinner' as it was often called. I had never heard

*Haydon's butcher's shop (right), Carshalton High Street, 1928*

of 'high tea' as eaten in the North until many years later.

I must admit that I am glad I am not one of the modern school-children with their synthetic protein 'meat' and fish fingers and 'whipped instant desserts', tasting of flavoured air, and as my parents and many of their contemporaries have lived into their eighties and nineties it does not seem to have harmed them to have enjoyed such splendid meals that today might be frowned upon by the experts. No doubt they led much more active lives, not being car-orientated, which acted as a counter-balance.

Home life certainly followed quite a set routine as certain nights were set aside for baths and hair-washing every week, plus a compulsory dose of the dreaded Syrup of Figs (I still shudder at the thought of that!). Every month I was taken by Mother to have my hair singed and trimmed at the barber's and hairdresser's known as Towersy & Brown in Ross Parade. This was an exciting event which I quite enjoyed, though it was a bit scarey when the lighted taper came close to one's face and one smelt the burning odour of hair! This practice has long since died out, but it was supposed to strengthen the hair. Later on, Marcel waving was performed by those two gentlemen for us, with hot tongs, and this continued until the revolutionary permanent waving was introduced in about the mid-thirties in our area.

This account of my everyday life would be incomplete without mentioning the advent of radio, and its exciting impact. We would rush home from school to listen to 'Children's Hour' and go into raptures over the popular band-leaders such as Jack Payne and Henry Hall while they were broadcasting. We were all very fond of the dance music of the day and Mother usually bought the songs to play on the piano. This in turn meant that I, for one, was specially popular at school, since I was able to play from memory for us to dance, when we were allowed (on wet days only) to spend part of the dinner-hour in the assembly hall. Periodically, however, this apparently innocent pastime was stopped, and looking back I now wonder whether it was in some way connected with the prevailing trend to have a 'crush' on certain senior pupils and teachers. Certainly at the time it seemed inexplicable to us and we were never given any reason for the ban.

Our main source of national and local news was, of course, the daily newspapers, of which we had two – the 'Daily Mail' which Father always took off folded under his arm to read during his train journey to the City; and the 'Daily Mirror' which he left behind for us to read at home. I adored the 'Pip, Squeak and Wilfred' animal cartoons therein, and also looked forward every week to my copy of 'Rainbow', the popular children's comic containing fascinating stories of 'The Bruin Boys' and 'Bluebell' (a schoolgirl character who, I think, wore a pair of magic gloves). Later on I changed over to 'Schoolgirl's Own' and revelled in the stories of life in boarding-schools with their high-minded heroines, fat girls and comic characters.

On the whole, I think that as children we were taken out with our parents far more than the modern child is. Daily walks to the shops or to relatives obviously took up more time, and involved personal contacts, rather than

**KENNARDS**
**MILL & FACTORY**
**SALE**

**November 2nd.**

Monday at 9.30 o'clock

KENNARDS' Factory Sale, which begins next Monday, is the greatest clearance sale of the whole year. It is not a clearance of retailers' stock such as takes place in January and June, but a clearance of the surplus stocks of hundreds of factories all over the country.

Kennards' Mill and Factory Sale is an annual event. Among the owners of mills and factories it has for many years been the recognised means of clearing their surplus stocks. Factories with stocks to clear send samples to Kennards in time for the Factory Sale. If the quality, quantity and price are right, Kennards pay cash for substantial discounts, with the result that the Factory Sale offers you clean, fresh merchandise, straight from the factories, at wonderful bargain prices, sometimes less than half the cost of manufacture.

**FATHER CHRISTMAS ARRIVES AT KENNARDS THIS SATURDAY, 11 o'clock**

WILL every child in Croydon pleass come to Kennards on Saturday at 11 o'clock in the morning to welcome Father Christmas? At 11 o'clock he arrives outside Kennards in the Treasure Ship loaded to the brim with sacks of toys, cases of toys, great boxes full of toys and the great big Golden Key which will unlock the door to Kennards Bazaar and the stores of joy and happiness the bazaar holds for all.

This is where you can see Father Christmas on Saturday. The best place will be at Kennards, but in case you cannot get there in time you can see him at Crystal Palace (Penge Entrance) at 9.15 a.m.; Penge at 9.30; Norwood Clock at 9.45; Selhurst at 10 a.m.; Gloster at 10.10; Thornton Heath Clock at 10.20; Thornton Heath Pond at 10.40; Croydon Hospital at 10.45; West Croydon at 10.50; and then at Kennards at 11 o'clock.

The Pipers Band will assemble at Broad Green to conduct the Procession to Kennards.

*Advertisement from The Sutton and Cheam Advertiser, 1931*

just being ferried to and fro in a few minutes by car, with mother concentrating on traffic and driving and so unable to draw attention to trees or flowers growing in gardens, for instance, or to stop and chat to friends and neighbours on the pavements. We also usually had to travel by tram or train into Croydon or Sutton to shop for special clothes, and this would involve having tea out in a large store such as Kennards (now Debenhams) in North End, Croydon, or the old coffee-house run by Wilsons, with its fascinating high-backed wooden seats and super freshly-ground coffee being roasted on the premises and served with cream and brown sugar and a special kind of biscuit. Toasted tea-cakes, hot buttered toast, or crumpets, would be chosen, to be followed by an array of fancy cakes served by waitresses in frilly aprons, and caps to match their brown dresses — and, at Kennards, all to the strains of light music from the inevitable trio or quartette, often of ladies only, hidden behind a bank of palms and plants.

I loved these outings, in my best hat and coat, as they made me feel quite grown-up, which was greatly encouraged by Father. Sometimes he would send me on an errand locally when I was quite small, such as round to Bute Road with a note to Mr. Knight, our somewhat old and crochety gardener, requesting him to come and cut the hedges. Another trip I had to do was to go up to the Gas Company's shop on the corner of Woodcote Road and Stanley Park Road and ask the Manager (a family friend) to supply me with 'one small inverted gas mantle, please' before the days of electricity. Another errand I always rather dreaded was having to go round to the old Council offices at 19 Belmont Road (site of the present Fire Station), where I had to ring a bell on the rather high old-fashioned counter and ask for 'Mr. Johnson, the Rates Officer, please', to whom I would then hand an envelope containing Father's rates. I had to be sure to bring back safely the precious receipt! Mr. Johnson, of course, spent many years serving the district, first with the Parish of Beddington and later with the Urban District of Beddington and Wallington, and eventually with the Borough of that name, retiring during the Second World War.

*Woodcote Road (1931), west side, just south of the railway bridge. The shops in the picture are those mentioned by the author. On the far left, Nobles, the chemist; then J. Short and Sons, dairy; H. Wise, pianos; J. Sainsbury; London and Suburban Meat Stores; Riddington's (café); Boots; Burnand and Pickett, builders; John Shaw; and Dixon & Co., estate agents.*

# CHAPTER FIVE

## *Shops and Shopkeepers*

If I close my eyes and concentrate, I can just about remember the old shops and shopkeepers of my childhood in Wallington, many of which remained the same until I grew up. Travelling from south to north of the parish, i.e., from Woodcote Green to Wallington Green, the wide tree-lined Woodcote Road up to the Stafford Road junction was the pride and joy of the district, since it consisted entirely of very large detached houses with splendid gardens and tennis-courts where several doctors and dentists lived, as well as Sir Richard Meller, our local M.P. Notable among the doctors was Dr. Peake, father of the artist and writer Mervyn Peake. Maid-servants and gardeners abounded in these residences, with sometimes a private chauffeur — as in the case of Mr. Ernest Hayes, a local author and publisher for whom I later worked as private secretary and assistant editor. As one looks at the present blocks of flats and empty sites it is difficult not to mourn the passing of this splendid road from its former glory.

Coming further down the road; when I was very young there were no shops until about Beddington Gardens, where Hepburns the corn chandlers had their crowded little shop on the corner and where the male staff always seemed snappy and awkward. Nobles the chemist's was a pleasant shop close by, and near to this was Short's Dairy where the buxom Miss Short was always cheery and talkative. Wise's music shop adjoined the dairy and was a favourite haunt of Mother in search of new songs to try over. I believe Sainsbury's was there from a fairly early date, with the high-class cake-shop and restaurant known as Riddington's a little lower down. This was a favourite rendezvous for ices or coffee on a Saturday morning while out shopping. On the other side of the main road the large draper's known as Aldis and Hutchings (later Tilley and Aldis and now the Post Office) held pride of place on the corner site. Before she was married, Mother was practically engaged to the son, Mr. Cyril Aldis, and we were always treated as V.I.P.s when we shopped there. I can well recall the head buyer Miss Atkinson coming forward when Mother entered the 'Baby Linen', for instance, and being given chairs to sit on while we made a leisurely selection of some tiny garment or other. Incidentally, the same treatment was given us when we shopped in Croydon at the large drapers known as Rowbotham's, where our family was also known to the owners. Shop-walkers, or buyers, as they were called, were very important people in their sphere and could command instant attention from their staff to look after a customer's needs. What a long way from the self-service and supermarkets of today!

Just below the railway there was a very tiny and quaint little florist's shop, more like a large greenhouse and cottage garden combined, called King's (see top picture page 29), which supplied all the flowers for weddings and funerals and various celebrations. Indeed they made all the bouquets for Mother's wedding in 1909 and also for my own wedding in 1939 — quite a record I would think. Sadly, when the railway station was modernised and the bridge eventually rebuilt, all this was swept away, though the florist's moved to another site and is still there today. Also tucked away under the bridge was the tiny sweet-shop owned by Mr. Waspe, frequently patronised by us when we had pocket-money to spend.

Railway Approach is firmly fixed in my mind as being the site of our family grocer's shop., Millest's, as Mr. Millest was the bane of my life because he was such a merciless tease, in addition to being bad-tempered very often. Mother and he would argue for hours or discuss local events and people on her visits to the shop about something that had gone wrong with the weekly orders, but if he were in a good mood he would let me select a few fancy biscuits from the large glass-fronted container-bins, since all biscuits were kept loose and weighed up into bags in the shop. This, of course, applied to almost everything, though sugar was often packed ready in dark blue bags. All bacon and cheese was cut on the counter, as also was butter which was patted into shape with two wooden platters before being wrapped and put into a bag.

A few yards further on we came to the shop of French, the photographers, who over the years took so many of the district's pictures, both personal and public; and indeed they also took the photographs for Mother's wedding and and my own, all those years later. Miss Mary French Kempsell, daughter of the proprietor, Harry French Kempsell, still lives in Wallington. When the shop closed in the 1950s, Miss Kempsell donated many negatives and prints of people, places and events in the locality, from the 1890s onwards, to Wallington Library. Some of them have been used to illustrate this book. Trotter's toy-shop and newsagents was situated in the middle of that parade and much visited by us as children for obvious reasons.

On the opposite side of the road various shops such as Shingle's dairy and Street's the greengrocers were patronised by us, and on the corner of Melbourne Road there was a large branch of the International Stores. In Mother's girlhood this had been privately owned by a Mr. Dobbie, whose daughter Elsie was one of her best friends to the end of their days, even surviving their removal to the then far-away Haywards Heath in Sussex!

Melbourne Road itself, apart from containing the public-house of that name, was quite often visited by me on an errand to Pannett's the butcher's. The butcher's two daughters, Kitty and Flora, were great friends of my Aunt Renée, and I would sometimes see one of them sitting at the desk in the back of the shop, making out accounts or giving change. Our one and only cinema at that time, 'The Gaiety', was to be found further along Melbourne Road, and was well patronised by us before the advent of The Odeon in later years. We had a lady to play the piano in those days of silent films, which added greatly to the emotional atmosphere of the dark and stuffy interior.

Pursuing my mental walk down Manor Road, there were several private houses on either side until one came to Brown the baker's on the corner of Park Gate Road, where the plump, rosy-cheeked Miss Brown was in charge of the shop and lived in the adjoining house with her blind sister. Their fancy cakes and delicious sticky buns of all kinds had to be tasted to be believed and have never been equalled in my experience since! On the corner of Queen's Road stood the large drapers known as Walls, presided over by a somewhat severe gentleman who expected good behaviour from us children when we had to visit the shop to buy our school uniforms.

Mother's parents were great personal friends of the Nelson family who owned the butcher's premises close by, and opposite the parish church of Holy Trinity there was the little old saddler's shop owned by Mr. Kelly and containing every item in leather that one could want. Johnson's yard and shop adjoined the end of that terrace and was a frequent haunt of mine in order to get a puncture mended on my bicycle, or some similar job done. Further down the long road there were various other small shops, mixed in with the beautiful Georgian, or older, houses still there, but we seldom ventured as far away from the centre as that, somewhat despising anything that was 'below the bridge'!

There were, of course, various other shops along the Stafford Road, but we personally did not frequent that area very often—though we did sometimes walk down to the Carshalton High Street shops, prominent among which was Haydon's the butchers, whose exciting two-wheeled box carts drawn by high-stepping hackney horses greatly enlivened our local streets on their daily deliveries round.

It will be realised from the foregoing that shops and shopkeepers formed a great part of my day-to-day life as a child, and for the most part the latter were counted as personal friends who watched one grow up and were always interested in the family and its doings; and I feel that life was certainly the richer for their being there, as compared with the barren impersonal approach of self-service and supermarket shopping at the present time.

*The author (left) with her two sisters Joan and Peggy in the garden of The Myrtles*

# CHAPTER SIX

*Illnesses and Treatments*

At the first sign of a cough or cold we children were kept away from school and tucked up warmly in bed, with the luxury in winter of a coal fire burning cosily in the bedroom grate. I can still recall the delight of watching dancing flames and shadows on walls and ceiling when the light was at last turned out. If influenza or tonsillitis were suspected, Dr. Cressy would be sent for and he usually prescribed the dreaded 'slops' which meant that we were to be given only such things as steamed fish, poached eggs, beef tea, milk puddings or jellies, and so on, until he called again in a day or so. Hothouse grapes generally arrived if one was seriously ill, as well as comics to read, and home-made barley water or lemonade to drink. None of your 'orange-flavoured' crudely-coloured squash that passes as a beverage today!

Many illnesses now regarded as mild and commonplace were real 'killers' when I was young, and it was not unusual for a child to die of scarlet fever, diphtheria or pneumonia — in fact I knew several children and adults who did. Modern antibiotics and inoculations have thankfully taken the dread out of many illnesses since then. Whooping-cough and measles, also chicken-pox, were quite dangerous complaints, and strict isolation periods had to be observed by all members of one's family.

At the tender age of six I had to spend six weeks away from home in the isolation hospital at Beddington because I contracted scarlet fever, and Mother was only allowed to view me through a glass door when she came to visit me. My main memory is of hearing some nearby hooter sounding the hour at noon with an intense shrieking noise, and being given what seemed like a non-stop diet of cold ham and boiled potatoes — most unsuitable for an invalid of that age with a fever and sore throat! Mother was allowed, however, to bring me jam, biscuits and fruit, so that helped to console me.

Then, when I was twelve, my sisters and I caught the dreaded diphtheria, but Mother refused to let us be sent away to hospital, so a trained nurse was engaged at great expense, and, between the two of them, plus the resident maid, we were nursed safely through the long weeks of fever. Disinfected

41

sheets had to be hung over the bedroom doors, all visitors had to wear white coats and face masks, and the whole house had to be fumigated by the local health officers at the end of the isolation period. Needless to say, there was no school for any of us for the whole of that term! People were endlessly kind with sending messages and gifts of fruit and flowers, since illness was quite a serious event then: I even remember hearing the news in hushed tones that straw had been spread over the road outside the house of one of my friends while he lay desperately fighting for his life with double pneumonia, in order that the noise of passing traffic should not disturb him until what was called 'the crisis' was past.

Of course there was no question of rushing out to find a chemist who could supply the doctor's prescription, as his own errand-boy would cycle up with the medicine bottles (never tablets then) after the evening surgery, since doctors made up most of their remedies on their premises and often in view of the patients. Tranquillisers and sleeping-tablets were virtually unknown, except in severe cases, when bromide or morphia might be administered. In cases of nerves or depression a strong iron tonic would be prescribed, with the advice to 'pull yourself together' and, lo and behold, it usually worked. At least we were not a nation practically addicted to drugs in some form or another as is the case now. Cod-liver oil and 'Virol' were favourite remedies for winter ailments; much to our disgust, as we hated the taste of these items. In fact we had very few things in our medicine chest in the bathroom, apart from fruit salts, cough mixture and liniments, plus iodine for cuts. The commonplace aspirin had not, I think, been invented at that time, and we certainly did not include it in our home remedies, having to endure headaches and other pains until they went away of their own accord. As for a visit to the local dentist (Mr. Sawday in Stafford Road) it was a point of honour to "be brave" and not cry out if there was pain — in contrast to the prevailing custom now of having injections to prevent every minor twinge of discomfort!

Thinking about ailments leads me to realise that there was very little social conscience about 'cripples' or orphans and others fallen by the way-side. Most places had their 'village idiot' who was often quite harmless, if eccentric or backward, and humoured by people; but such modern terms as spina bifida, spastic, autistic and so on were quite unknown to us, or the conditions to which they refer understood. The thing that most moved me personally was hearing about the terrible state of lepers in far-away countries where the missionaries were apparently the only people trying to relieve their sad fate. How different today when so many of these conditions can be controlled, if not cured, and when every schoolchild can help to raise funds for the many good causes sponsored by television programmes or national charities, and are so much more aware of the Third World and its problems. Reverting to orphans, one of the highlights of an afternoon walk in Wallington for me as a child would be to catch a glimpse of 'the little orphans' as we called them; namely, the children from Beddington Orphanage of famous origin, housed in what is now called Carew Manor, who added a touch of drama to the scene by always wearing long coloured cloaks and bonnets when they were allowed out on occasional shopping expeditions, under supervision of course. I fear I did not at the time realise the sadness of their situation, as compared with the comforts of my own home.

A Cart Load of Orphan Girls from the Royal Female Orphan Asylum, Beddington.
French & Co.-Photographers, Wallington.

*Orphans: an early 20th Century postcard*

*The Girls County School, Wallington, attended by the author, and previously by her mother, when it was situated in Queens Road, Wallington.*

# CHAPTER SEVEN

## Schooldays

At the age of six I was taken to my first school at 'Southview' in Elgin Road, a pleasant private establishment run by two spinster ladies, Miss Styles and Miss Reid, with the aid of one or two other youngish teachers. There were no such things as Play Groups for pre-school toddlers, so it was all a wonderful new experience for me and I was happy from the start. After a few days of going to and fro with Mother, one of the older pupils was detailed to shepherd me as she lived quite near, and this went on until I was old enough to go on my own. I must have made quite good progress, since at the age of about eleven I passed the Entrance Examination to the local County Grammar School, where I remained until I was seventeen.

The building then in use was the same as that to which my mother had gone as a girl, situated in Queen's Road, with a narrow entrance to the headmistress's study from the Manor Road side. It was very old-fashioned as to heating and general accommodation, with what was called a 'covered-way' leading from one set of classrooms to another. There was an asphalt playground which was also used for netball, and this led through to what was virtually the school tuck-shop, a little old place where we often spent our pocket-money before or after school on such favourites as sherbet-fountains, liquorice ribbons, or chocolate drops. For some reason which I was never able to fathom, Mother did not like us to have sherbet sweets, perhaps on medical grounds; nevertheless I often indulged myself and prayed that nothing nasty would befall me!

In my final years at school we were immensely excited at the news that a wonderful modern new school was to be built for us in Stanley Park Road, with extensive playing fields and every possible item of the latest equipment, as well as a splendid large assembly hall with parquet flooring and a specially-built house for a resident caretaker and his family. (This school is now situated in an even newer building at Woodcote Green.) By this time I was in the Sixth Form, working hard for examinations, and it was a high-spot of the summer term for us as seniors to be allowed to work outdoors under

45

the shady trees in the spacious grounds.

Those were very happy years and I made several good friends, notably 'the two Margarets' (Margaret Kimber, who still lives in Wallington, and Margaret Keslake, who lived in Sandy Lane, and now lives at Goring-on-Sea) with whom I am still in close contact: quite an achievement in an era of great change and mobility, not to mention the intervention of another world war. All our school-mistresses were fully qualified and would appear in their caps and gowns at the annual prizegivings, where all pupils had to wear white dresses and sat in a segregated block, well away from parents.

It was, of course, compulsory to wear school uniform, which in our case consisted of navy-blue serge tunics over cream blouses or woollen jerseys, with striped green silk ties and waist girdles, under which we mostly wore grey woollen bloomers and black stockings! In winter, we wore outdoors a navy-blue reefer coat (very expensive) with black velours hat and badge. In summer one felt very dashing in dark navy-blue blazer with badge on pocket and cream panama hat — although later on we were introduced, as a special concession, to check cotton summer dresses and what were known as sun-tan lisle or silk stockings. Plimsolls were only allowed to be worn for games or gymnasium lessons — somewhat different from the present cult of teen-agers all wearing old and dirty plimsolls all year round for walking outdoors. I think we should have nearly died of shame if we had not been able to appear in the regulation black leather shoes, with lighter slippers to change into before entering the classrooms!

As to discipline — woe betide any girl seen to be behaving badly or noisily in public transport, or not wearing her hat in the street, since this would surely be reported by a mistress or prefect, with dire consequences such as a visit to the headmistress's study and loss of privileges. Worst of all, any girl seen fraternising with boys, perhaps by going on the back of a motor-bike or bicycle, could risk being expelled by the headmistress, Miss Wallace, who ruled the school with an iron will and was supported in this by all parents. I personally cannot recall any specific cases of violent bullying, such as occur today in girls' and comprehensive schools, though of course certain mistresses and other pupils could make one's life unhappy for various reasons. Our school motto was 'Self-knowledge, self-reverence and self-control' and the code of honour was very strict, forbidding the telling of tales or cheating in any form whatsoever. Vandalism was quite unknown.

All in all, however, we had a lot of fun before we settled down in time to work in earnest for our matriculation examinations. For French lessons we had a genuine French mademoiselle, while singing, music and cookery were taught by experts. Netball and hockey in winter, alternating with tennis and cricket in summer, were the order of the day. Visits to the nearest swimming baths, in Sutton or Croydon, were not often organised, but we went along with friends during the holidays or week-ends and were taught to swim by the resident instructor. Homework was a heavy burden as one grew older, and I recall staggering home with my attaché-case crammed full of books and files every week-day, with extra for the week-end; but at least there was no television to prevent one from concentrating if one so desired.

I remained at school until I was seventeen, as I have said, and am not ashamed to admit that on my last day I was in tears at the thought of that part of my life coming to an end. I am still grateful for the splendid education that I received, which must have formed the basis for whatever talents I later developed; though I did not realise it at the time.

*Fire drill at the Wallington County School for Girls, Stanley Park Road. In October 1928 this building replaced the earlier one in Queens Road.*

*The author as a
baby, on holiday
with her mother
and a friend*

*Paddling at
Bognor Regis - 1927*

48

# CHAPTER EIGHT

## Holidays

The natural progression from schooldays is to holidays, of which we had several during the year, but of course the great excitement was the annual summer vacation, to be spent usually at the sea or in the country. The first sign of the approaching exodus would be two enormous cabin trunks being brought down from the loft and placed on the landing. Mother and the maid would then spend every spare hour washing and ironing our summer dresses and petticoats, and packing them between layers of tissue paper into the trunks — quite a formidable task since there were we three girls, plus mother and father, and it was customary to take a wide selection of coats and hats and dresses, to say nothing of bathing costumes, sandals, mackintoshes and umbrellas, and so on, to cover all types of weather possible in the normal English summer.

The night before our departure, all the household silver and valuables, together with pets, would be taken round to Normanhurst for safe keeping by the grandparents during our absence. When I was very young I can recall this trip being done in a horse-drawn cab, but later on we had a hired car to take us round to Grosvenor Road, and also to transport us all the way to the South Coast; until the time came when we owned our own family car, one of the early Morris Cowleys.

I never enjoyed these journeys because I was invariably sick at intervals (this being long before the boon of travel sickness pills), so I was thankful when we finally arrived at Eastbourne, Worthing or Bognor Regis, as the choice might be, and drew up at the boarding-house or private apartments Mother had arranged. Generally the maid came with us, as already mentioned, so as to give my parents plenty of freedom in the evenings to go off to concert parties or listen to the band, which was the great event twice daily on the promenade.

Punch-and-Judy shows were a great source of pleasure for us when the tide was high and we could not play on the beach. There was also a man who made the most wonderful patterns and castles on the sands, to say nothing of the Lady Diver in Flames who jumped off the end of the pier twice daily, watched by an admiring but fearful crowd.

On holiday, Father always prided himself on getting up in time to take us out for a brisk walk before breakfast, in order to collect the newspapers. The menu for that meal would be about the same as at home, with the addition of porridge, if desired, and coffee as an alternative to tea. During the morning we would mostly adjourn to the beach and, if at all possible, would paddle or bathe; but a strict ritual had to be observed which involved only about ten or fifteen minutes in the sea, in case we caught cold, and a prompt rub down with rough towels the minute we came out of the water — followed by sticky buns and lemonade to keep our strength up! Parents would have to undress and dry off in the seclusion of a bathing-machine in those very early days. Sun-bathing, as such, had not been thought of, so we were quickly re-dressed in our summer frocks and sandals and taken back to mid-day dinner. 'Bed and Breakfast' was unknown to us, full board being given as normal practice.

In the afternoons there might be an excursion to some notable place of interest, on foot or by charabanc, but always there was a break for after-noon tea, and we had to be sure of returning in good time to wash and change into a clean dress for the evening meal of several courses. Television being unknown then, the holiday-makers usually went out to a concert or theatre for the rest of the evening, or settled down in the drawing-room with the rest of the company to read, write letters, or play cards.

Camping or caravan holidays were unknown to us, apart from scout or guide camps, and indeed Mother would have scorned such arrangements, since she expected to be waited-on and cooked-for on her holidays, and part of the general enjoyment was to dress up in various different clothes during the day according to the activities involved.

When I grew into my 'teens we had progressed from the South Coast further afield to Dorset, Devonshire, Somerset and finally Cornwall, where we spent so many deliriously happy holidays amidst scenery that was so new to us and so lovely that we never wanted to return to our suburban roads and houses. Each evening our parents would take us for long drives through the narrow lanes with their high hedges, and we loved to see the emerald fields on the cliff-tops running so often right down to the sandy coves below. And it was quite rare to see another car, so the feeling of peace and tranquillity was complete.

Package tours to foreign countries and non-stop sunshine were unheard-of, and ordinary families seldom went abroad, so these more remote parts of our own island were a revelation in themselves, and nothing can erase the memories of those childhood holidays when the simple pleasures of shell-collecting and 'shrimping' in warm pools of sea water were first discovered. Quite often we were the only family to be staying as visitors in the village of St. Blazey near Par, and formed lasting friendships with our hosts; and I recall with delight the huge bowls of Cornish cream at every meal.

50

# CHAPTER NINE

*Pastimes and Pleasures*

Memories of holidays lead naturally on to recollections of how we spent our evenings and week-ends, and of course this really *was* the period of 'Anyone for tennis?' since everyone belonged to some kind of tennis or cricket club, and played badminton indoors in the winter months. It was unthinkable not to wear all white clothes on these occasions (dresses for girls and long flannels for men), and most clubs possessed a small pavilion where dances were held on Saturday nights to the music of a local amateur band. This was a happy meeting-ground for girls and boys to be properly introduced to each other, and many an engagement and marriage followed in the natural course of things. It was quite usual, too, for residents with large gardens to have a private tennis-court marked out on a side-lawn, and I often went up to play thus at the house of a friend at Sunnybank in Woodcote Road, later to become the site of the new Town Hall. I daresay many of us did not ever play tennis really well, but we certainly enjoyed ourselves, and doubtless the exercise in the fresh air was good for us anyway.

There was also usually a branch of the Conservative Association, or a Junior Municipal League, which held regular meetings with debates and lectures. Dramatic and operatic societies abounded for those with acting or musical talents; and all these groups held regular dances at the local halls, with admission by tickets only, and full evening dress required from both sexes! When I see the modern teenagers drifting off to their local disco or youth club, in their patched, ragged and dirty jeans, and T-shirts and plim-solls, I feel quite sorry for them that they have never known the joy of saving up for, and choosing, really pretty evening dresses in lace or net, with silver slippers and fresh flowers for a corsage. In fact, choosing new dresses for the summer, and coats and hats for the winter, took up quite a lot of our spare time and gave immense pleasure, since the materials were very colourful and varied; and if one had to visit the dressmaker to have such things personally made, this took up several hours and involved patient standing during the various fitting sessions. Satin or crépe-de-chine lace-trimmed underclothes were also much admired and saved-up for, especially the quite extensive trousseau which it was usual for brides to acquire.

During my schooldays, in common with many children, I attended dancing classes privately twice a week at the establishment run by the Misses Gardener in Springfield Road where it adjoins Manor Road; also a gymnasium class on Saturday mornings. Periodically there would be 'a display' which involved Mother in the making of special costumes for dances such as the Irish Jig, the Rose Dance, the Sailor's Hornpipe, the Scottish Sword Dance, or Welsh Reel; also the purchase of my much-loved Bronze Slippers, as compared with the plain black we wore for weekly practice sessions. The Rose Dance was my favourite, as I wore a very dainty dress of white flounced net, sprinkled with tiny rose-buds and forget-me-nots, and carried a little basket full of those flowers, with also a wreath on my hair. Artificial flowers in those days were quite exquisite pieces of work, being of silk or velvet, and I think largely made by hand, for the trimming of hats, as compared with the stiff mass-produced plastic 'blooms' of today.

As I grew older, these lessons were replaced by evening Music Lessons given by Miss Rimington of Ross Road, and I cannot help recalling how happily and fearlessly I would trot off after tea, complete with music case, and return in the dusk, with never the thought or experience of vandalism or assault to mar my innocent excursions. How sadly different is the scene today when it is hardly possible for a child to walk or cycle alone in town or country in complete safety from attack from sexual deviants, to say nothing of the enormous traffic hazards.

Cycling was, in fact, another of our most popular pastimes, and in the holidays several friends would go off to the nearby downs at Chipstead and pick primroses, wild daffodils, or bluebells and cowslips in the woods. We would hardly meet anyone else, so there was no question of leaving the land bare of plants. With a bottle of fizzy lemonade or ginger-beer to cool us down and quench our thirst, we would freewheel joyfully down the hills and trudge up the other side, hoping to arrive home before the lovely flowers faded.

Sundays were mostly taken care of in those early days by going to church morning and evening, and to Sunday-school in the afternoon; but as we grew older our parents liked to take us out for a drive in the afternoon, and it became very fashionable to try out the various new road-houses or country cottages where cream teas would be served, catering for the growing number of motorists visiting the countryside at the week-ends; which I suppose was the beginning of the great decline in Sunday observance and church attendance.

Our year was punctuated at regular intervals by such national events as the Oxford and Cambridge Boat Race in the Spring, the bonfires and fireworks for November 5th, and the great climax of Christmas. On Boat Race day everyone, and I mean everyone, wore a favour of dark or light blue, and it was a point of honour never to change sides in one's support of either crew. Outings by train or coach were often arranged to take parties of children and parents to the riverside, and the excitement was quite intense until the result was officially declared.

The same attitude prevailed for the Guy Fawkes celebrations, when every garden boasted its small bonfire and display of fireworks, plus an enormous public blaze laid on by the Crusaders (a church youth movement) on a piece of waste ground between The Drive and Stratton Avenue. But I think I can truthfully say that I cannot remember a single occasion when anyone was hurt or frightened on those nights, because we mostly left it to the adults to purchase and light the fireworks and tend the bonfires, and paid attention to the instructions and warnings of those in charge.

Christmas was largely the same family occasion as at present, but the shops were never full of decorations and presents for so many weeks beforehand as in modern years. In our case we all went round to Normanhurst for Christmas Day and met up with the various aunts, uncles and cousins, all sitting down at the huge table with its leaves pulled out for the main event of the day, the turkey and Christmas pudding meal. In the afternoon we were expected to play quietly with our presents while the grown-ups dozed; then afternoon tea would appear, with the traditional large iced cake and other goodies; after which we would all gather in the drawing-room for a 'musical evening' with songs at the piano and everyone expected to 'do a turn', especially the children, who were coaxed into brief dances or recitations. As I grew older I was allowed to stay up later and join in the card games, which ended when the elaborate cold supper would appear around nine or ten o'clock. Cold turkey, with York ham and salad, would be followed by trifles, jellies, hot mince pies (all with lashings of whipped cream); followed in turn by fresh tangerines, grapes and crystallised fruits, and finally glasses of sweet port-wine to sip with the walnuts and brazils.

Best dresses and suits were definitely the order of the day, and one of the highspots was when the ten grandchildren were called in to be given a shining silver half-crown by Grandfather, only 12½p. in today's currency, but it seemed like a fortune to a child of the Twenties, and was much appreciated. How grown-up I felt, in my red velvet dress and gold locket, returning home about midnight, tired out with all the eating and excitement!

In contrast, the next day, being Boxing Day, was usually somewhat of a disaster, as it was Mother's birthday and she nearly always seemed to wake up in a bad temper with the feeling of being done out of a normal birthday's celebrations because of its coinciding with the Christmas festivities. Nine times out of ten she would find fault with whatever present Father had bought for her, and there would be quarrels and tears; but I would try to keep out of the way and enjoy playing with my presents and eating the silver-papered tangerine and tiny pink and white sugar mice that had been found in my Christmas stocking. Best of all, I could begin to read one of the books that had been given to me, often by Grandmother, and lose myself in another world. 'Little Women' and 'What Katy Did' were read time and again over the years, until I knew them by heart, likewise the very sad and horrific tales told by Hans Andersen or the Brothers Grimm. 'Cranford' and 'Daddy-Longlegs' were two other special favourites, and I worked my way steadily through the Scarlet Pimpernel series, probably laying the foundations unconsciously for my life-long love of the printed word.

I must not conclude this chapter on pleasures and pastimes without mentioning the fact that, as time went by, visits to the theatre and cinema were regular events, especially with a new boy-friend; and every town boasted at least one cinema where we were transported into an enchanted world of romance and adventure as portrayed by the great film stars of the thirties. Organ interludes were a great feature of the larger cinemas in Croydon and Sutton, and long queues of people would form outside, especially on a Saturday evening, waiting for tickets to enter the warm darkness of escapism.

# CHAPTER TEN

## *Religion*

Looking back on a lifetime of active membership of the Church of England, I am conscious of gratitude for the fact that I was sent off to Sunday-school at an early age, followed in due time by confirmation into the adult church. Actually, my first memory of a church was being taken at Christmas time by 'Old Uncle Ben' (I was about six years old) to St. Mary's, Beddington, for the special purpose of seeing the golden Infant Jesus in his crib – I think it was a life-size replica and this made a great impression on me.

We were fortunate in having, at Holy Trinity Church in Wallington, for most of my youth, an outstanding preacher in our vicar, the Rev. the O'Shea of Kerry, to give him his full title; and to this day I recall many of his admonitions and phrases. The fact that we also had a rather handsome curate as well, no doubt added to the pleasure of church attendance, since I spent much of my youth falling in love with various members of the opposite sex!

Thinking back to the congregation at that time, I can still picture the two Miss Gurneys who lived in one of the nearby large houses in Manor Road, and who came to church in winter swathed in grey squirrel fur coats and smelt deliciously of expensive 'Attar of Roses' scent on their lace-edged handkerchiefs. A little further along Manor Road lived the really eccentric lady of Wallington: namely, Miss Pill, who was always dressed completely in black from head to foot and wore her extremely long hair piled up about a foot high under her bonnet. She occasionally had an Indian missionary to stay in the house (well chaperoned by two resident maids, of course) and this was a point of great interest locally since it was almost unheard-of to see an Indian or an African in our neighbourhood. Major Pothecary with his family (the daughter Ruth being a close friend of mine) also attended the church, and was, I think, the main solicitor in our community then. Holy Trinity was always what one would call a 'middle of the road' church, being neither too 'high' nor too 'low' in its approach. Great store was set on this, particularly as the trend in the parish church at Carshalton was to be Roman Catholic in all but name; with St. Michael's in Milton Road being nearly as 'high' and much frowned on by the great majority. There was, of course, a great deal of religious intolerance at that time and Ecumenism had not been thought of.

At the time I am speaking of, the 'Crusaders' movement was very popular among young people, and much sought after, although at this distance I realise it had a great snob value. The prevailing strict rule of membership that only admitted children from grammar or public schools did not then strike me as at all unsuitable or unchristian. Indeed, I was very proud to be admitted to the select band of girls who gathered for Bible readings and the singing of 'choruses' every Sunday afternoon in a private house. I suspect that the occasional meetings at what we called 'squashes' with the boy Crusaders in their own new hall in Stanley Park Road had something to do with the attraction also!

It was more or less automatic to be confirmed as one entered one's teens, but I still recall the sense of dedication and awe that I felt, as, dressed in white from head to foot, I was received into the Church of England and blessed by the then very old Bishop of Woolwich in the ancient church at Beddington on a spring evening during 1928. The avenue of enormously tall trees lining the road to the old church met overhead and created a vault of greenery and arching boughs which added greatly to the atmosphere surrounding the peaceful churchyard, where many of my own relatives were buried. Mother often told the tale of how her own grandfather would walk to that church every Sunday morning, carrying a tiny posy of flowers from the garden at Sunnydale under his top hat, to be placed on his wife's grave in the ancient churchyard.

We had a Young People's Fellowship attached to the parish church, and this met every Monday evening in the draughty and dingy parish hall in Queen's Road for various talks and games or socials. Apart, however, from an occasional garden fête in summer for Dr. Barnardo's Homes, I cannot remember any social or charity events in connection with our church life, and obviously religion was largely to be reserved for Sundays and not carried over to weekdays! The only event every year which remains in my mind is the Armistice (now called Remembrance Day) service which was held at Wallington Green by the War Memorial and attended by huge crowds in a very emotional atmosphere. Later I became a Sunday-school teacher at the Elm Grove Mission nearby.

Not very much emphasis was given to the special festivals of the Christian Year as regards floral decorations or discussions, though the sermons carried suitable messages appropriate to the day; but the richness of the liturgy and music added much to one's inner experience. As for myself, I believe that the ideals of the Christian way of life are beyond compare, and personal faith an anchor to cling to. But oh, what a hard path it is to tread, and no wonder so few even attempt it!

# CHAPTER ELEVEN

## Manners and Customs

The suburban society of Outer London when I was young was an unbelievably enclosed and exclusive one. There was a fine degree of snobbishness as regards which road you lived in, which school you attended, what your father did for a living (factory work was non-existent in our immediate area and practically every father travelled daily to the City to an office job of some kind or other); and, most of all, your accent — upper class, middle class, or just plain 'common'. We seldom heard an Irish, Scottish or North-country voice, and almost never a foreign one. In fact, even as late as 1939 when the Poles arrived at the beginning of the Second World War they might have been inhabitants from another planet!

The same parochialism applied to visiting (or even knowing about) other parts of London, especially those on the opposite bank of the Thames. It was a major expedition to travel to the suburbs on those other sides of London, and seldom undertaken. Even places like Mitcham, Brixton, Islington, the East End and so on were spoken of with aversion and to be avoided whenever possible — quite different from the present time when it is the 'in' thing to live right in the heart of the Metropolis, never mind how derelict or ancient the property.

It was, of course, really a crime to be poor (regardless of the cause) and as there was no such thing as a benign Welfare State to succour such unfortunates, there must have been numberless cases of real suffering and starvation. Neither can I recall such events as modern coffee mornings, jumble sales, wine and cheese evenings, barbecues and so on which are held now to help so many deserving causes. Doctors. dentists, solicitors, and other professional men were definitely looked up to. Membership of the local golf or cricket clubs was somewhat difficult to obtain as it was rather a "closed shop" affair. Most of one's friends' fathers worked in the Civil Service in London, or the Bank, or in some City firm, and there would be a daily stream of them walking to and from the station, since cars were pretty rare. Despite the absence of traffic, though, it was quite unthinkable for children to play out in the streets where we lived, as neighbours would have complained, and it was socially unacceptable, so we always stayed in the garden, apart from an occasional ride on our scooters or fairy-cycles on the pavement outside the house.

Likewise, drinking in public-houses was just 'not done', especially for women and girls; but most homes had whisky or other spirits and wine in the sideboard cupboard, and for many years the American craze for cocktails was widespread, involving the greatly-prized cocktail cabinet which soon became a 'must' in the furniture of most houses. Swearing as such was non-existent among polite society as compared with today, and such words as 'bloody', 'Christ' (used as an expletive) and so on, were so rare as to be almost blasphemous. Table manners were carefully taught to small children and it was a matter of personal pride to hold and use one's knife, fork and spoon elegantly, in strong contrast to the present trend of 'shovelling' things into the mouth so often depicted in the television commercials as done by all ages. 'Please' and 'thank you' were certainly heard much more often, and it was customary for a child to write a pleasant thank-you letter for any gift received at Christmas or birthday. We were always taught never to take the best or largest of any item offered, or to put ourselves forward before others — but then this was all before the days of modern psychology which seems to me to teach only the pursuit of happiness and self-expression, and never mind who goes under in the process.

As regards fashion, we did tend to be slaves of whatever current trend was in vogue, as, for instance, the craze for knitted silk jumpers, ultra-low waists, cloche hats and two-tone shoes — all greatly admired in the twenties. Make-up was quite limited: being mostly a 'vanishing' cream and a dusting of loose powder, with a discreet touch of lipstick — but certainly nothing like eye-shadow, mascara, bright nail varnish, hair-spray or deodorant. Enamel or gilt solid powder-compacts were very popular for a long time, and I can just recall hiding one in my desk while still at school and surreptitiously dabbing my shiny face with the minute puff before I went home, no doubt in case I met my current boy-friend on the way! It would, of course, have been confiscated had it come to the notice of my form-mistress.

In this connection, I must admit that physical beauty as such was greatly admired and cultivated at that time, and it was almost a crime to be what was termed 'plain' or to have straight hair. Hence the enormous popularity of the permanent wave when it was invented. A good skin, large eyes, well-shaped nails, slender ankles, to say nothing of a good figure — all these things added up to, I suppose, one's potential value in the marriage market, as it was assumed that all men preferred these assets rather than such abstract things as talent or personality.

All of which leads me to reflect that our sex-life was expected to be (and generally was) almost non-existent before marriage, and certainly abortions or illegitimate babies were never heard of in our circle. We certainly had numerous boy-friends and there was plenty of scope after dances or tennis parties, so perhaps our very innocence and lack of knowledge protected us from disasters! Girls and boys alike seemed to know by instinct the limits to be imposed in any love-making, even during the longish engagements which were normal. Possibly we missed a lot, but it did not seem to worry us. The same approach was true of drugs, pornography and homosexuality, none of which ever entered our world so we were unaware of many of the problems such as beset the youth of today.

The one thing that was strictly followed right up to the Second World War was the custom of wearing black for long periods of mourning after family bereavements, but this custom died out after the war-time clothes rationing made it quite impossible. Previously, regardless of expense, near relatives were expected to buy complete outfits in black, and the period of full mourning was followed by a period of half-mourning when mauve was permissible. Black armbands were worn for more distant relations. Wreaths and floral designs for funerals were very elaborate, in great contrast to the simple tributes or donations to charities which many people prefer in these days of cremation and inflationary prices.

Almost the biggest change that strikes me, looking back, is that when I was young we were always trying to appear, and to be, grown-up, whereas now the trend and cult is to stay young and student-like for as long as possible. There were no special teenage clothes, so the transition from childhood to maturity was quickly accomplished and was something to be looked forward to as soon as schooldays were over. There was an increasing tendency for girls as well as boys to think about training for a career, but apart from secretarial work or teaching, there was not much scope. Certainly it was unthinkable in our circle to serve in a shop or be a waitress! I wonder if the young people today value the complete freedom they now possess in this respect alone? Most girls, like myself, really had at the back of their minds the ultimate goal of marriage and babies, and any job was more in the nature of providing pin-money for clothes than as a career or to provide a living, since it was out of the question to live away from one's home in a flat in the modern style. And I doubt whether any of the boys I knew would have been able to boil an egg or make tea in a place of their own, let alone cope with their washing and shopping! We certainly were helpless and spoilt in that sense.

No record of the legendary Thirties would be complete without some reference to the Great Depression and the tragic unemployment that resulted − but, to be honest, I cannot recall that it affected any of my immediate circle of family and friends. Nor was I conscious of these events on a National scale. The only thing I do remember vividly was the General Strike in 1926, which we all thought rather exciting and a little bit frightening − but it was soon forgotten once life returned to normal.

The outstanding national event at Christmas for many years was the speech made by King George V on the new 'wireless', and we all listened in awed silence to this modern miracle which brought the King's gruff voice into our homes. I also recall watching on warm June evenings from the front garden for the royal party to drive past our house in Park Lane on their way back from the Derby and Oaks races at nearby Epsom. Later on, when we had our own family car, we were always taken up to the course to wander round the old-style gypsy caravans which crowded on the Downs the night before the race meetings, and we greatly enjoyed the general excitement with all the fun of the fair and having our fortunes told.

Old people's homes as such were unknown when I was young, since most grandparents stayed on in their own homes, with usually an unmarried daughter to act as housekeeper when they became too old to cope; or else they went to live with one of their married children and gradually became absorbed into the family life there, as houses were much larger and room could more easily be found for an extra person or two.

Another change that has taken place is the difference in the general street scene, because then people all wore proper coats in varying colours and styles, according to season, with matching or toning hats. In summer such hats would be very pretty with bunches of shiny artificial cherries or wreaths of poppies and cornflowers adding colour and texture to the many types of straw shapes available. Fur coats or trimmings were greatly admired and acted as a sort of status symbol. No one gave a thought to the deaths of the animals, and this is one area of modern thought which has greatly changed for the better, I am thankful to admit; but the contemporary street scene strikes me as terribly dull and boring with the eternal faded blue jeans and T-shirts and plimsolls for all.

# CHAPTER TWELVE

## Game, Set and Match

One of the great events in the social scene was the celebration of one's twenty-first birthday and coming-of-age, when all one's family and friends attended a full-scale party or dance, either at home or in a local hall, each bringing the customary expensive gift.

It was soon after this occasion that I met my husband-to-be, Dennis Whiteing, in a very conventional way, namely, at a meeting of the local debating society. He was in fact one of the young men in Mr. Johnson's Rating Office, and, apart from war service, spent over thirty years in the service of the local authority. After a year's friendship we became engaged officially, and I still remember how thrilled and proud I was to be wearing my diamond ring for the first time.

Wallington had, of course, been gradually changing and developing during the years of which I have written, and a new Town Hall had by this time been erected in Woodcote Road and the town had been granted borough status. The airport had also been established on the Croydon boundary: it might have been called Wallington Aerodrome had it not been for the doubts and objections of the local people and council in case it led to a deterioration of the district. But of course the aircraft incorporated in the coats of arms of the original Beddington and Wallington Corporation, and the present London Borough of Sutton, commemorates this fact, which is of special interest now that the airfield has been redeveloped.

Reverting to my engagement, I was, myself, during this period working as assistant editor to the firm of publishers (the Religious Education Press Ltd.) formed by the author Mr. Ernest H. Hayes, of Woodcote Road, for whom I worked for ten years after leaving school; the offices later occupying the premises of the old Post Office in Manor Road. During the next eighteen months my fiancé and I both saved very hard in order to fill the traditional 'bottom drawer' and to buy the necessary furniture and furnishings for our future home. It was out of the question to start married life then on second-hand bits and pieces, though after the Second World War this became a

61

*The author's wedding to Dennis Whiteing at Holy Trinity Church, Wallington, on April 8th, 1939. The group includes, from left to right – the bridegroom's parents (Mr. & Mrs. Whiteing), Margaret Keslake, Kenneth Searle, the bride and groom, Joan Lawrence, Margaret Kimber, Peggy Lawrence, and Mr. & Mrs. Lawrence, the bride's parents.*

necessity through the long years of shortages. Recently I came across an old scrapbook in which I had noted down the amounts and costs of such things as carpets and curtains, and was amused to read that the price per yard for the latter was (in old money) about three shillings — or at the time of writing now, about fifteen new pence!

Our budget to start married life in our modern rented maisonette was carefully planned-out to total £4 per week, and this included the rent and rates for the very pleasant living accommodation and small garden; housekeeping and laundry; light, fuel and gas; clothes and amusements, and insurances! I find it almost impossible to believe this, but have written evidence to prove it is true!

Even my white lace wedding-dress, complete with three-foot train, was made (by the dressmaker Ann Beaufort of the Arcade in Sutton) for around three pounds, with hand-finished satin bindings and minute satin buttons specially made. Looking through my old diaries recently, I found the exact details of the wedding reception for seventy guests in Stewarts' Restaurant, Woodcote Road. The price for the upstairs hall was to be £1, and this included a sit-down meal with waitress service, plus all crockery, glasses and flowers on the tables! The menu read as follows:-

Sandwiches (various fillings)
Sausage Rolls
Lobster Patties
Fruit Jellies or Fruit Salad
Meringues and Cream
Coffee, Lemonade, Orangeade
Fancy Cakes and Tea to be served at the close.

And all this for the unbelievable sum of three shillings per head — 15 new pence today!

Our wedding was fixed for early April and the actual day proved to be one of brilliant sunshine and blue skies. The service at Holy Trinity was fully choral, bells and all, and my four bridesmaids (sisters Joan and Peggy and the two Margarets) looked delightful in their pale green organdie full-skirted dresses with lilies-of-the-valley in their hair. I shall never forget the glorious scent of my 'shower' bouquet delivered early in the morning from King's the florists, as it was composed entirely of white roses, lilies, carnations and gardenias. Our parents and guests were dressed to the hilt, dripping with picture hats, fur wraps and jewels! And in the early evening the 'radiant couple' left by train from East Croydon for their honeymoon at Eastbourne — a favourite resort at that time — amid clouds of confetti and cries of good luck.

In fact, there was only the one cloud to cast its shadow on the day — the year happened to be 1939. So it was not only the end of the Thirties but the end of an era, for, five months after our wedding, the sirens sounded shortly after the Second World War was declared, and overnight our lives

63

were completely changed.

Within a year or so, my husband was a member of the Royal Air Force, our precious new home was put into storage 'for the duration', and the tennis courts disappeared into allotments, as we stifled our fears and once more added a stiff upper lip to our physical equipment, with a silent prayer for victory and survival.

With gratitude to those who sacrificed their lives, I can happily record that all my friends and relatives did survive; but at the end of it all nothing was ever the same again, and it seemed impossible to pick up the threads to make the same pattern. So my story of times remembered comes to its end — a story I have tried to record with honesty, kindness and affection, to show truly the good and the bad of that unique period in our small corner of Surrey as I knew it.